# Good Health Naturally

*Promoting, Maintaining and Restoring Health God's Way*

by

Bertha M. Baber

**RoseDogBooks**
PITTSBURGH, PENNSYLVANIA 15222

The contents of this work including, but not limited to, the accuracy of events, people, and places depicted; opinions expressed; permission to use previously published materials included; and any advice given or actions advocated are solely the work of the author, who indemnifies the publisher against any claims stemming from publication of the work.

The information presented in this book is for educational purposes only. It is not intended to replace proper medical diagnosis or treatment by a medical doctor or health care practitioner. The author is not liable for any claims resulting from the information or the applicatioin thereof.

*All Rights Reserved*
Copyright © 2008 by Bertha M. Baber
No part of this book may be reproduced or transmitted
in any form or by any means, electronic or mechanical,
including photocopying, recording, or by any information
storage and retrieval system without permission in
writing from the author.

ISBN: 978-0-8059-8623-5
Printed in the United States of America

*First Printing*

For more information or to order additional books,
please contact:
RoseDog Books
701 Smithfield Street
Third Floor
Pittsburgh, Pennsylvania 15222
U.S.A.
1-800-834-1803
*www.rosedogbookstore.com*

## Appreciation and Gratitude

In appreciation of a loving God who placed in our environment all of the things which we need for long life and good health.

With special gratitude to my husband, Warren, who helped me in many ways during the writing of this book and to my sister, Brenda Seymour, who typed the original manuscript.

# *Contents*

Introduction . . . . . . . . . . . . . . . . . . . . . . . . . . . . . . . 1
The Bible Speaks on Good Health . . . . . . . . . . . . . . . . . . 3
Some Reasons For Not Being in Good Health . . . . . . . . 5
God's Eight Natural Health Principles . . . . . . . . . . . . . . . 6
Reasons to Be Aware of These Principles . . . . . . . . . . . . 6
Natural Health Principles . . . . . . . . . . . . . . . . . . . . . . . 8
    1. Sunlight . . . . . . . . . . . . . . . . . . . . . . . . . . . . . 8
    2. Exercise . . . . . . . . . . . . . . . . . . . . . . . . . . . . 10
    3. Sleep and Rest . . . . . . . . . . . . . . . . . . . . . . . 13
           Ways to Promote Rest and Relaxation . . . . . . . 15
           Stress Management . . . . . . . . . . . . . . . . . . . . 15
    4. Fresh Air . . . . . . . . . . . . . . . . . . . . . . . . . . . 18
    5. Pure Water . . . . . . . . . . . . . . . . . . . . . . . . . 21
    6. Nutrition . . . . . . . . . . . . . . . . . . . . . . . . . . 24
           Factors that Determine the Effectiveness of Diet
           and Nutrition . . . . . . . . . . . . . . . . . . . . . . . 24
           Guidelines for Meal-Planning . . . . . . . . . . . . 27
           Food Groups . . . . . . . . . . . . . . . . . . . . . . . . 29
           Properly Preparing Vegetables . . . . . . . . . . . . 29
           Fruits and Vegetables Extend Our Lifespan . . . 31
           Whole-Grain Foods . . . . . . . . . . . . . . . . . . . 34
           Protein in the Diet . . . . . . . . . . . . . . . . . . . 36
           Flesh Foods in the Diet . . . . . . . . . . . . . . . . 37
           The Importance of Proper Food Combining . . 40
           Food Combining Chart . . . . . . . . . . . . . . . . 43

7. Temperance and Intemperate Eating Habits ..... 44
8. Trust in God .............................. 46
Personal Notes ................................ 47
Personal Health Chart ......................... 49
Health Diary .................................. 51

# Introduction

Health is a state of mental and physical well-being. It is the absence of disease. Today, many people are becoming more health conscious, and they are seeking knowledge that will help them to assume greater responsibility for their own health. They are no longer contented with just treating the symptoms of sickness and disease. They want to know what causes these conditions and how to prevent them as well as how to treat them. The answer lies in how to become truly healthy.

There is no such thing as a quick-fix for poor health, but there are principles that promote health and help to prevent sickness and disease. They also help to reverse ill-health if the body has not deteriorated beyond help. No one thing will achieve good health, but rather a combination of principles and practices which form a healthy lifestyle that will result in good or improved health. The source of these principles is God. As our Creator, He knows exactly what we need for optimal health and peak performance.

The purpose of this manual is to give an understanding of these principles and related information in order to help others both understand what a healthy lifestyle is and to realize that it is the true basis for all good health.

Some of the definitions given by Webster's Dictionary for the word principle as it is used throughout this book are (1) the cause of something, (2) a natural endowment from nature (endowment: syn.-gift, provision, benefit) and (3) the law by which a thing operates.

For many, to adapt to some of these principles will require a degree of change in lifestyle, and it may be helpful to gradually change by practicing only a few new principles at a time.

Remember, persistence and faithfulness in necessary change will be greatly rewarded in terms of good and improved health, physical fitness, appearance and general outlook on life.

If you are interested in being healthy and staying that way, continue to read, my friend. You have nothing to lose and everything to gain!

# The Bible Speaks on Good Health

1. "A merry heart maketh a cheerful countenance: but by sorrow of the heart the spirit is broken." (Prov. 15:13)
2. "Pleasant words are as an honeycomb, sweet to the soul, and health to the bones." (Prov. 16:24)
3. "A merry heart doeth good like a medicine: but a broken spirit drieth the bones." (Prov. 17:22)
4. "Heaviness in the heart of man maketh it stoop: but a good word maketh it glad." (Prov. 12:25)
5. "The merciful man doeth good to his own soul: but he that is cruel troubleth his own flesh." (Prov. 11:17)
6. "Hope deferred maketh the heart sick..." (Prov. 13:12)
7. "Be not wise in thine own eyes: fear the Lord, and depart from evil. It shall be health to thy navel, and marrow to thy bones." (Prov. 3:7, 8)
8. "There is that speaketh like the piercings of a sword: but the tongue of the wise is health." (Prov. 12:18)
9. "A sound heart is the life of the flesh: but envy the rottenness of the bones." (Prov. 14:30)
10. "Blessed art thou, O land, when...thy princes eat...for strength and not for drunkenness!" (Eccl. 10:17)
11. "The sleep of a laboring man is sweet..." (Eccl. 5:12)
12. "...let not the sun go down upon your wrath:" (Eph. 4:26)
13. "It is vain for you to rise up early, to sit up late, to eat the bread of sorrows: for so he giveth his beloved sleep." (Ps. 127:2)

14. "Come unto me, all ye that labour and are heavy laden, and I will give you rest."  (Matt. 11:28)

\* These verses have been taken from the King James Version of the Bible.

## Some Reasons for not Being in Good Health

1. Hereditary illnesses
2. Unhealthy lifestyles that have been learned or passed down through families and society
3. The pollution of our environment
4. Violation of health principles due to ignorance, economics, lack of time, negligence etc.
5. Lack of proper medical attention
6. Stress due to various circumstances
7. Accidents
8. Weakened condition of the human race since the fall of Adam and Eve
9. Sin and separation from God
10. Any combination of the above

The good news is that we can eliminate some of these negative health factors from our lives and reduce the effects of others upon us. More sickness and disease are attributed to unhealthy hereditary lifestyles than to hereditary illnesses themselves. This information is encouraging because it lets us know that by changing unhealthy aspects of our lives, we may also change and improve our health. Let's read ahead and see how this is possible!

# God's Eight Natural Health Principles

1. SUNLIGHT
2. EXERCISE
3. SLEEP AND REST
4. FRESH AIR
5. PURE WATER
6. NUTRITION
7. TEMPERANCE
8. TRUST IN GOD

These principles are the means through which God works to sustain human life and health. They are effective because they were created by God who is life and health. He created them personally by the power of His word. They are not within man's jurisdiction in that they are not the product of man's manufacturing or concocting. They are part of a once perfect environment that God created on earth to sustain the life which He placed there. As man's Creator, God intended man's life and health to be dependent upon Him and His principles.

## REASONS TO BE AWARE OF THESE PRINCIPLES
1. To learn what is best for our bodies by realizing that the God who created us knows best what we require for maximum health and performance
2. To understand that our God is a God of principle and order, and He has created our bodies to function in an orderly manner based upon the principles of His design
3. To obey God because He has ordained that *we* should properly care for our bodies (I Cor. 3:6-17; 6:19,20; 10:31)
4. That we might enjoy good health longer

5. That we may help and encourage those who are not in good health
6. By both understanding and regarding these principles, we may benefit to a greater or lesser degree in the following ways:

   A. Maintain good health
   B. Prevent, delay or reverse illness
   C. Lessen suffering or the severity of illness
   D. Keep the illness under control
   E. Recuperate more quickly
   F. Look and feel better
   G. Be more productive

# Natural Health Principles

## 1. SUNLIGHT

Unfortunately, there are people who are extremely sensitive to sunlight and cannot tolerate it; but, for those who can, it is a great tonic for whatever seems to ail you! Its wonderful light and heat are only a few of its many life and health supporting properties. Human life cannot exist without sunlight. Many studies have given evidence to the following information.

### BENEFITS OF SUNLIGHT

1. Sunlight is used in photosynthesis for the making of green plants which supply food, protection and beauty for man.
2. Sunlight plays a vital role in the earth's water cycle.
3. Dampness, mold and mildew (which cause sickness and disease) can be prevented and cleared by keeping the area exposed to sunlight as much as possible.
4. Sunlight aids in mental depression, anxiety and stress by lifting the morale and by giving a sense of well-being.
5. The ultraviolet rays kill harmful bacteria on the skin.
6. The ultraviolet rays help the body by converting the cholesterol under the skin to vitamin D for healthy bones.
7. Moderate and regular exposure to sunlight increases both the oxygen content and the number of white blood cells in the blood, improves blood circulation, lowers the respiratory

rate, helps wounds to heal better and faster, aids in lowering and maintaining excessively high blood sugar levels and strengthens the body's overall immune system making it more resistant to sickness and disease.

## SUNSENSE!

1. The sun's ultraviolet rays are the most intense between the hours of 10:00 A.M. and 3:00 P.M. If possible, we should avoid the sun during these hours or be sun-protected by wearing hats, scarves, sunglasses, sunscreens and light-colored clothing to reflect the sun's rays.
2. We should begin sun exposure by only a few minutes each day and gradually increase the time by a few minutes every several days.
3. We should never remain in the sun too long, and overexposure should be especially avoided if one is sick or weak.
4. Care should be taken not to fall asleep when sunbathing.
5. The intensity and effect of the sun's rays are about the same on cloudy, overcast days as on bright, sunny days; and the same precautions should be taken.
6. We may benefit by being in either direct or indirect sunlight.

## 2. EXERCISE

As the old saying goes, "We were made to wear out, not to rust out." Would you like to look better, feel better and possibly live longer? Try moderate, routine exercise! The body was made for activity, and it does not respond well to a sedentary lifestyle. The modern "couch-potato" lifestyle contributes to many major health problems such as heart disease, high blood pressure, diabetes, osteoporosis and obesity. The body uses routine exercise to help prevent and control these conditions.

### WHAT FAITHFUL EXERCISE CAN DO FOR YOU

1. Exercise helps you to relax, to sleep better, and to better tolerate the stress of everyday living.
2. Routine exercise improves the tone of the muscles and blood vessels by changing them from weak, flabby tissue to strong, firm tissue. Lack of exercise results in weak, flabby, atrophied muscles and weak bones.
3. The lungs become more efficient by processing more air with less effort.
4. The heart is made more efficient by becoming stronger and pumping more blood with each stroke. Thus, the number of strokes is reduced, and you are able to do more work with less fatigue.
5. Regular exercise increases both the number and size of blood vessels and the total blood volume. This process saturates the tissues of the entire body with more energy giving oxygen. By increasing maximum oxygen consumption, the overall condition of the body is improved giving it protection against many sicknesses and diseases.
6. Being physically fit enables a person to develop a better self-image.

7. Faithful exercise gives you quicker reaction times and increases both energy and endurance levels.
8. Routine exercise helps to build denser bones by helping the body to produce more calcium.
9. Consistent exercise creates lean body mass while burning fat.
10. Lack of exercise leads to abnormal and accelerated blood clotting in coronary, cerebral and other arteries and veins, increasing the risk of heart attack and stroke.
11. Walking is the best overall physical exercise. Many studies now report that running and jogging are not good forms of exercise as the constant pounding and jarring cause shock and trauma to the body's joints. This will ruin and wear them out. The joints especially effected are the knees and the ankles. Better forms of exercise include housework, gardening, swimming and bicycling.
12. Exercise must be regular, vigorous enough and sufficiently prolonged to be of benefit.
13. Try not to study or do heavy exercise immediately after eating as it overtaxes the body.
14. When confined to a bed or chair, the body may be exercised by just moving the head, neck, shoulders, arms, legs, hands and feet.
15. When work requires sitting for long periods of time, stand up and move about periodically.
16. It is not necessary to overtax the body for long periods of time. It is the faithfulness of routine exercise that pays off. The body can greatly benefit by exercising several times a week from fifteen minutes to an hour.
17. Some people enjoy the quiet, private time alone to exercise. Others are motivated by exercising with another person or in a group.
18. Keep well-hydrated while exercising, and stop if you begin to feel ill in any way.

19. Always allow time to warm up before exercising and time to cool down before stopping.
20. For best results, try to exercise outdoors in the fresh air with good deep breathing.
21. Over age fifty, be careful and avoid jumping, pounding exercises.
22. Check overall health before starting any exercise program and begin slowly and gradually.
23. All of the factors listed above help to slow the aging process and physical deterioration. They contribute to health, a sense of well-being and longevity.

## 3. SLEEP AND REST

The human body is wonderfully made, but it can malfunction, break down and wear out prematurely without proper care. One important aspect of this care is getting sufficient sleep. We cannot expect to function well by subjecting ourselves to long hours of stress and work each day while allowing only a few hours of sleep each night. Many people go without sufficient sleep, but it is only to their detriment. In order to be at our best, our "batteries" need to be recharged regularly. This is done by getting ample sleep each night or on a regular schedule.

### REJUVENATING, HEALING SLEEP

1. The body heals and repairs itself during sleep.
2. Certain important hormones such as the growth hormone are released only during sleep.
3. Sleep relaxes the muscles and rids them of waste materials such as uric acid.
4. It is the lack of proper sleep and rest while you are well that causes you to become sick.
5. Proper sleep and rest produce a more cheerful disposition and provide strength for the next day.
6. Proper sleep and rest reduce stress, anxiety, tiredness and irritability.
7. Lack of sleep and rest make one more susceptible to sickness and disease as it weakens the entire immune system.
8. Insufficient sleep and rest make one more accident prone as the brain is not as alert as it should be; and therefore, does not function as well as it should.
9. Sufficient sleep and rest prevent premature aging, lines and wrinkles in the face, circles around the eyes and poor general health.
10. Studies show that the hours of sleep before midnight are

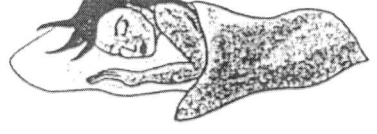

more beneficial than those after midnight. One hour of sleep before midnight is equivalent to two hours of sleep after midnight.
11. Go to bed and get up at the same time each day to train the body.
12. Shut out light for maximum benefit of sleep.
13. Keep area ventilated, but avoid drafts.
14. Sleep is rest and the body needs mental and physical rest regularly.
15. Try not to eat more than several hours before bedtime in order to allow the stomach to rest.
16. Sleep and rest keep the brain sharp and alert.
17. Plan for seven to eight hours of sleep each night. Studies and reports now reveal that most Americans suffer from a lack of sleep. These reports indicate that many traffic accidents and fender-benders are the result of people falling asleep at the wheel. Many employers are concerned about poor work performance from employees who are tired and sleepy on the job. A great number of students underachieve and often fall asleep in class due to insufficient sleep and rest. Not everyone requires the same amount of sleep, but many authorities today feel that the body does not function well on six or less hours of sleep each night. Seven or eight hours are better. According to studies, when the body has not received enough sleep at night, it periodically "snatches" very short periods of sleep throughout the day. The person is not usually aware that he has actually slept for a few seconds. Such is often the case in car accidents and accidents on the job. It is not uncommon for people to function not fully alert and nearly asleep on their feet. Bad attitudes and irritability often result from sleep deprivation.
18. For those who have difficulty sleeping, they should have

their overall health checked, slow down the lifestyle, resolve problems, get enough physical activity during the day to be tired enough to rest at night, wind down before bedtime and free the mind of all activity.

## WAYS TO PROMOTE REST AND RELAXATION
1. Get moderate exercise routinely.
2. Try a change of pace.
3. Bathe in tepid water.
4. Enjoy a relaxing amusement.
5. Listen to relaxing music.
6. Do something thoughtful, kind or helpful for someone else.
7. Read a good book.
8. Keep area ventilated.
9. Love and enjoy life.
10. Have a peaceful, grateful and contented heart.
11. Find peace with God, and spend time with Him daily.
12. Stop all work at a certain time each day. Allow time to wind down and to relax.
13. Neither place nor receive phone calls after a certain time of day unless it is really necessary.
14. Plan one or more short intervals throughout the day during which you may simply sit down alone quietly in a comfortable position and relax.
15. Learn to manage personal stress.

## STRESS MANAGEMENT
Stress robs the body of proper sleep, rest and good health. Stress upsets the delicate chemical balances within the body leaving it susceptible to mental and physical disorders. Medical science now realizes that stress is the underlying cause for nearly all major sickness and disease. Serious, long-standing, unresolved

problems destroy the body's natural ability to cope with stress. When this happens, the immune system is weakened; hence, various organs and systems of the body begin to wear out and shut down, resulting in major mental and physical illnesses of all kinds. People may react differently when stressed, but no one is immune to the negative effects of stress, especially when it is prolonged and unwanted.

We live in a stressful world, and we cannot eliminate all stress from our lives; however, it is in our best interest to both reduce and properly manage stress as much as possible. The following are some good ideas for helping with stress management:

1. Identify the problem and set up a plan to either eliminate it or to control it in order to reduce its effects upon you.
2. Practice being more positive by stopping, thinking and changing negative thoughts and comments to more positive ones.
3. Look for the good and the positive in life.
4. Associate with more positive and supportive people.
5. Be organized and timely. Plan ahead and avoid rushing and last minute plans.
6. Be realistic in setting goals and expectations for yourself and others. Don't set yourself up for failure by setting too difficult or impossible goals.
7. Create a pleasant, relaxed, stress-free environment.
8. Have some quiet time alone each day.
9. Eat a good diet and eliminate or limit caffeine products.
10. Practice deep breathing daily.
11. Get ample sleep and routine exercise. Have enough activity during the day to be tired enough to sleep at night.
12. Rectify and avoid problems and misunderstandings with others as much as possible.
13. Avoid prolonged worry and anxiety.

14. See to any personal health problems.
15. Slow down the lifestyle, and learn to do only one thing at a time.
16. Become aware of and educated on the topic of stress.
17. Don't be afraid or feel badly to say "no" when asked to do something that you are not able to do or don't want to do. Don't allow yourself to be dumped on or intimidated.
18. Don't be fearful of expressing your true emotional feelings at difficult times.
19. Realize when silence is golden.
20. Have a trusting relationship with God, and share your stresses with Him.

## 4. FRESH AIR

The layer of air that surrounds the earth is called the atmosphere. It consists of many gases including oxygen and carbon dioxide. These two gases support plant and animal life on planet Earth. When we exhale, carbon dioxide passes from our lungs into the air where it is absorbed by plants. The plants use the carbon from the carbon dioxide to help produce plant food (carbohydrates) and release the oxygen back into the air. When we inhale, our lungs take in the air and remove the oxygen from it to sustain our lives. Oxygen is food for the body. Sufficient oxygen is required for life and quality health.

### FRESH AIR AND GOOD HEALTH

1. The air we breathe is about 20 percent oxygen. As our lungs filter oxygen from the air, circulating blood in the lungs absorbs the oxygen and carries it to every cell throughout the body.
2. Every cell in the body needs a constant supply of oxygen or it will weaken or die. Air must be fresh to help you the most. Stale or polluted air does not supply enough oxygen to keep the cells strong and healthy.
3. To assist the lungs in processing as much oxygen from the air as possible, we should practice slow, deep breathing until it becomes natural. When one shallow breathes, the poisonous wastes which would be given off are retained in the body and the blood becomes impure. Thus, the entire body with its organs and systems is negatively affected.
4. Good respiration soothes the nerves, stimulates appetite and helps to induce sound sleep.
5. Deep breathing helps to stop pain and relaxes the entire system.
6. Plenty of fresh air is essential in helping to prevent and

treat upper respiratory problems such as colds, flu, bronchitis and tuberculosis.
7. Oxygen from the air helps the body to purify the blood.
8. Shade trees and shrubbery which are too close and too dense around the house block the purifying air and sunlight. They promote dampness and prevent good air circulation around the house.
9. Do not rent or buy homes in low lying damp areas as such damp places induce sickness and disease. Research studies by the National Institute of Health in Washington County, Virginia, in the late 1950s and early 1960s substantiated these facts and revealed that homes built in such places frequently had a history of cancer in those who lived in them. This included homes along creeks, narrow valley bottoms and rivers as the continually flowing air picks up the dampness more so than in elevated places.
10. Smog is quite harmful. Much smog is from cars and vehicles.
11. It is now known that fallen tree leaves, which remain ungathered, give off carbon monoxide fumes which poison the air.
12. Well-documented studies give evidence to the following facts regarding the importance of oxygen in the body to heart disease and illness:
    a. Lack of oxygen in the system is one of the causes of hardening of the arteries.
    b. As the fat content in the diet is increased, the amount of oxygen in the tissues decreases.
    c. By increasing the amount of oxygen breathed, hardening of the arteries may be prevented or reversed, especially when combined with a low fat diet.
    d. Lack of sufficient oxygen in the body tissues weakens the immune system leaving the body more susceptible to sickness and disease.

    e. Many chronic degenerative diseases may be traced to a lack of sufficient oxygen in the tissues.
13. Remember that poor diet and stress deplete the body of oxygen.
14. Our homes should be constantly ventilated with fresh air to replace oxygen that is used up as we breathe and to recondition the air from the use of aerosols, cooking and heating of our homes.
15. Some time should be spent outdoors in the fresh air everyday.
16. When possible, live in the country or in the suburbs in order to have cleaner air and to escape some of the city air pollution.

## 5. PURE WATER

Water is the most important part of a proper diet because it is necessary for all body functions. About 80 percent of the body is water, and without sufficient water there can be no life, growth or healing. The body can go longer without food than without water, and it benefits from the proper use of water, both internally and externally.

## WATER AND THE HUMAN BODY

1. Since 80 percent of the body is water, to lose as little as 10 percent of body fluid is serious, and 20 percent loss is fatal.
2. A person should drink at least one-half the number of his pounds in weight in ounces of pure water each day. Ex. If you weigh 160 pounds, you should drink 80 oz. of water or 10-8 oz. glasses daily.
3. Even a physically inactive adult uses up to 8-8 oz. glasses of water daily because water is the medium for virtually all of the body's chemistry, and it is used constantly.
4. About 90 percent of the blood is water. Water in the blood carries oxygen and nutrients to every cell in the body and carries waste products away from the cells.
5. Sufficient water keeps the blood thinned properly and flowing with less difficulty. As a result, the heart doesn't need to work as hard.
6. The flowing blood maintains the delicate chemical balances in the body, its organs and systems.
7. Common constipation, backache and headaches can often be relieved by drinking enough water at regular times.
8. Water is a lubricant preventing friction between the body's joints and muscles in the same way that oil prevents friction between machinery parts.
9. During manual labor and many strenuous sports, the body is

stretched, twisted and bent in ways that wouldn't be possible if water weren't present.
10. Water is used in hydrotherapy to relieve pain and to promote healing.
11. Bathing eliminates toxins, increases blood circulation, relaxes the muscles and soothes the nerves. Impurities not washed from the outside skin are reabsorbed by the body creating internal problems.
12. Lack of sufficient water results in dehydration which is the cause of many physical disorders. By the time one feels thirsty, he is already somewhat dehydrated.
13. Extra water is needed during sports activities and prolonged exercise in order to prevent dehydration and to reduce stress on the circulatory system.
14. The body is cooled by the evaporation of water from the skin (perspiration). Water also equalizes body temperature by transporting heat from one part of the body to another through circulating fluids. These processes regulate and maintain proper body temperature. They also safeguard against overheating, heat exhaustion and possible strokes.
15. During illness, greater water intake helps to regulate body temperature and to control fever.
16. Water intake can increase physical endurance by 80 percent.
17. The more salt, sugar and protein that we eat, the more water we need to process them.
18. Weight loss is made easier by drinking ample water.
19. The body cannot use food in its solid form. Water is used in the process of digestion whereby the food is broken down into a liquid state. This liquid passes through the walls of the intestine into the bloodstream where the nutrients are absorbed and carried to the tissues of the body. Insufficient water in the system results in poor

digestion and malabsorption of nutrients.
20. The kidneys need water, water, water to do the work of cleansing the blood by filtering waste products and impurities from it (including the residues from medicines). This removal of impurities keeps the body from becoming toxic and prevents the wastes from building up or settling in one place causing complications. Insufficient water in the system overtaxes and ruins the kidneys contributing to poor function or failure of them. Continued accumulation of wastes in the kidneys as a result of poor function, sets the stage for inflammation of the bladder (cystitis) and bladder cancer. Doctors may restrict water intake during certain illnesses.
21. Urine is the fluid which carries the waste products from the kidneys to the bladder. As the bladder fills, the waste products (urine) are excreted from the body. Dark urine indicates illness or not enough water in the system. Healthy urine should be pale.
22. "Water and sanitation is one of the primary drivers of public health. I often refer to it as "Health 101", which means that once we can secure access to clean water and to adequate sanitation facilities for all people, irrespective of the difference in their living conditions, a huge battle against all kinds of diseases will be won." *Facts & Figures Updated* - Nov., 2004. Dr. Lee Jong-Wook, Director-General, World Health Organization.

# 6. NUTRITION

It is now known and well-documented that diet plays a crucial role in both health and disease. Needless to say, we are beginning to realize a few very important principles: (1) Your life and health are dependent upon the nutrients that your body digests and assimilates from the food that you eat. (2) People are digging their own graves with their teeth. (3) Our food is also to be our medicine. (4) An ounce of prevention is worth a pound of cure. (5) Many medical problems are not so much hereditary as they are the result of learned and hereditary lifestyles. (6) We cannot enjoy good health while living in violation of the principles which sustain it.

Now, that we as a society, realize these things, we are applying the knowledge by reeducating ourselves on how to develop a healthy dietary lifestyle. The information presented in this section and the section on Meal-Planning serves as a guideline for helping us.

## FACTORS THAT DETERMINE THE EFFECTIVENESS OF DIET AND NUTRITION

1. Forty percent or more of the diet should consist of raw foods in order to provide maximum nutrition for the body.
2. Combine foods properly and avoid overeating to prevent fermentation and putrification in the colon.
3. Eat the heaviest meals early in the day, and try not to eat before bedtime to maintain healthy body weight and to allow the digestive system to rest at night.
4. Don't eat when angry or stressed as this interferes with the production of enzymes needed for the proper digestion of food.

5. It is best not to drink liquids with meals as the liquids interfere with digestion by diluting the digestive enzymes. Drink no less than thirty minutes before or after a meal.
6. Try to eat at the same times each day as the body functions best on a schedule, and it will prepare to release the digestive enzymes at the accustomed times each day.
7. Eat slowly and chew food thoroughly to aid digestion. Digestion begins with the mixing of the enzymes in the saliva with the food in the mouth.
8. Meal times should be pleasant times. Leave unpleasant things for another time as emotional upsets slow and stop digestion.
9. Prepare food attractively.
10. All fried foods should be eliminated as grease and unhealthy oils interfere with digestion and the absorption of nutrients in the body. They also clog the system, especially the arteries. When heated to high temperatures, grease and oil form harmful toxins which are released into the body when eaten.
11. Eliminate all processed, prepared and canned foods as they usually lack good nutrition and contain harmful preservatives, color additives and high levels of salt.
12. Foods in the order of their greatest to least nutritional values are fresh, frozen, home-canned and commercially canned goods.
13. Eat a well-balanced and varied diet for maximum nutrition and good health.
14. A well-balanced and varied vegetarian diet provides ample protein.
15. Avoid foods containing preservatives, coloring and additives as these things are associated with sickness and disease-especially cancer.
16. Oil should be consumed as found naturally in foods such as avocados, olives and nuts. Hydrogenated oil (solid) should

never be used as it clogs the blood vessels. Unsaturated oils are preferred.
17. Avoid excessive protein in the diet as it overworks the organs (especially the heart and kidneys), promotes sickness and disease and shortens life.
18. Avoid heavily-spiced foods, sugar and excessive salt and oil as they often cause digestive problems and other health disorders.
19. Rotate foods by not eating the same food more than every four days to prevent boredom in the diet, promote good health and prevent food allergies from developing.
20. Overcooking food destroys texture, ruins color and destroys the vitamins and minerals.
21. Food should be prepared in large pieces as the cutting of food destroys its nutritional value.
22. Avoid using, eating or drinking from all aluminum cookware, utensils or containers. The use of aluminum has been associated with sickness and disease, especially Alzheimer's Disease.
23. The diet should consist of vegetables, fruits, grains, beans, peas, seeds, nuts and water.
24. Sickness and disease often begin in the colon as the result of poor dietary habits, ongoing poor digestion, dehydration and poor bowel habits.
25. Make sure the bowels move daily to eliminate toxins and waste products.
26. If able, periodic fasting allows the body to rest, cleanse and heal. There are many types of fasting programs.
27. Eliminate or reduce coffee, tea, tobacco and alcohol because of the negative effects upon the body from the caffeine content.
28. Be aware that many people are allergic to corn, wheat, dairy and soy products.

## GUIDELINES FOR MEAL-PLANNING

1. Establish regular times for meals as the body anticipates and prepares for these times.
2. Have several varieties of whole grains each day in the form of breads, cereals and special dishes. They are a good source of complex carbohydrates, amino-acids, fiber and the B-Vitamins. Breads may be in the form of waffles, muffins, French toast, bagels, cornbread, pita pockets etc.
3. Plan for at least three to four vegetables each day, and be certain to include the dark green leafy ones regularly. They include collard, kale and turnip greens, spinach, Swiss chard and various lettuces. These vegetables are high in nutrition and help to protect against heart disease and cancer. Romaine is one of the most nutritional lettuces; iceberg lettuce contains very little nutrition.
4. Include plenty of vegetables from the cruciferous group. They include cabbage, Brussels sprouts and broccoli. These are known as anti-cancer foods.
5. Allow for at least two to three fresh fruits daily - one citrus. They are high in vitamins, minerals and fiber. They also greatly protect against cancer.
6. White potatoes are lower in nutrition than many vegetables.
7. Plan to serve as many raw fruits and vegetables as possible for maximum nutrition. Steamed vegetables are best if the digestive system will not tolerate them raw.
8. Include both dark green and yellow vegetables in each main meal.
9. Place beans or other legumes in the menu three to four times a week. They are an excellent source of harmless protein.
10. Limit rich foods and plan sparingly for seeds, nuts, nut butters and avocados because of their high fat and oil con-

tent. If you do not digest seeds and nuts well, put them into a blender to make nut milk to be used in recipes that call for milk.

11. Fruit juices and concentrated foods should be planned in small amounts. It is better to eat the whole fruit than to drink fruit juices as the pulp provides dietary fiber which aids in digestion and prevents the fruit sugar from being absorbed into the bloodstream too quickly.

12. Never combine heavy proteins and starches in one meal such as beans and potatoes. They don't digest well together.

13. Plan no snacks between meals, unless it is a special diet, so that the digestive organs may rest.

14. Foods should be harmless, nutritious, fairly easy to prepare and look, smell and taste good.

15. Vary the textures, colors and flavors of foods within a meal to spark interest and taste.

16. For health's sake, use salt, sugar and oils sparingly.

17. Avoid fermented, old and spoiled foods. Three days old, without freezing, should be the limit in order to prevent eating contaminated food.

18. Eliminate processed, canned, boxed and refined foods such as white bread, pasta and rice. These foods have the nutrition processed from them. Canned and boxed foods have little nutrition, are high in sodium and contain colorings, preservatives and various chemicals.

19. For those who eat meat, it should be eaten in small amounts and no more than several times a week.

20. Vary the foods from meal to meal, but don't have too many varieties at one meal.

21. Fruits and vegetables should not be combined in one meal as the body does not digest them well together.

22. The last meal of the day should not be too heavy, and it should be eaten several hours before bedtime.

23. Adjust meals to meet the individual needs depending upon a person's budget, lifestyle, work schedule, type of work, climate, special health needs and taste.

## FOOD GROUPS
### Balancing the Diet

The diet should be balanced by eating a variety of foods from each one of the food groups listed below.

<u>Vegetarian Diet</u>
Fruits
Grains
Vegetables
Legumes (beans and peas), seeds and nuts

<u>Non-Vegetarian Diet</u>
Fruits
Grains
Vegetables
Legumes (beans and peas), seeds and nuts
Meat/Poultry
Dairy

*The first four food groups listed in the non-vegetarian diet should comprise the greatest part of the diet.

## PROPERLY PREPARING VEGETABLES

1. Avoid using bruised or wilted vegetables.
2. Vegetables should be cleaned and properly stored in the freezer or refrigerator for immediate use.
3. Use a plastic scouring pad or a stiff brush to clean vegetables.

4. Clean or rinse vegetables quickly. Avoid holding them long under running water or soaking them as many of their vitamins and minerals are water-soluble and can be washed away.
5. Soaps and detergents should not be used to clean vegetables. Residues from these cleaning agents are harmful and may be absorbed by the vegetables or remain on them. There are commercial preparations which are made especially to help remove chemicals and pesticides from fruits and vegetables when needed.
6. Keep vegetables cold until ready to cook.
7. Fresh raw vegetables may be juiced in a juicing machine. The juice contains the greatest amount of nutrition possible from the vegetables. It requires no digestion and the nutrients are absorbed directly into the bloodstream. These juices should be consumed slowly and immediately after juicing. Vegetable juices are often used to help restore health to those who are sick and "run down".
8. Vegetables are healthiest when simply cleaned and eaten raw or used in raw vegetable recipes.
9. Some people prefer cooked vegetables or have difficulty eating raw ones. For them (and for special recipes), vegetables may be juiced, steamed, baked or broiled.
10. To preserve nutrients and color when steaming, start vegetables in boiling water and cook uncovered for one minute. Cover, reduce heat to lowest setting and cook until fork tender. Use both as little water and cooking time as possible. To keep from wasting the nutrients, drink the remaining liquid or use it in a recipe instead of throwing it away.
11. When possible, cook vegetables whole or in large pieces and with the skins on to preserve the nutrients. Remove all green thick patches of skin from potatoes.

12. Vegetables should not be fried or have grease or oil added to them. Grease and oil interfere with the body's ability to properly digest food and absorb its nutrients.
13. Do not stir vigorously and stir as little as possible.
14. Cook vegetables just before serving. Keeping them warm after cooking causes loss of food value because they continue to cook. If they must wait, allow them to cool, then reheat.
15. Cooked vegetables should have a crisp, tender texture. When overcooked, they are mushy, strong-flavored and lose nutrition and natural color.
16. Avoid using utensils that are chipped, worn, have copper alloys or are made of aluminum.

## FRUITS AND VEGETABLES EXTEND OUR LIFESPAN

At a press conference in Washington, on July 1, 1992, Louis W. Sullivan, M.D., secretary of Health and Human Services, announced the National Cancer Institute's five-year commitment to encourage Americans to eat more fruits and vegetables each day.

"Research clearly shows that a diet with plenty of fruits and vegetables is good for health, but Americans are not reaching the basic goal of five or more servings daily," Dr. Sullivan said. "Improving our diets may have a significant impact on reducing cancer risk and making us healthier."

In launching the NCI's "5 A Day For Better Health Program," the agency defines a serving size as one medium fruit, six ounces (3/4 cup) of 100 percent fruit or vegetable juice, one-half cup cooked or raw vegetables or fruit, one cup of raw leafy vegetables or one-fourth cup dried fruit.

A great number of studies have shown that a diet rich in fruits and vegetables can protect against cancer, said Peter Greenwald, M.D., Dr. P.H., director of NCI's Division of Cancer Prevention and Control. These studies conclude that people with high fruit and vegetable intake have about half the risk for many types of cancer as people with low intakes. It is important to remember that a lack of a single serving each day may add up to a great deficit over time, he said.

In addition to eating five or more servings of fruits and vegetables daily, the NCI program recommends a low-fat, high-fiber diet as a way of maintaining health.

The NCI and other government agencies also suggest you:

- Eat a variety of foods.
- Maintain a healthy weight.
- Use sugars in moderation.
- Use salt and sodium in moderation.
- Reduce fat intake to 30 percent or less of total calories.
- Increase fiber intake to 20 to 30 g. a day with an upper limit of 35 g.
- Consume alcoholic beverages in moderation, if at all.
- Minimize consumption of salt-cured, salt-pickled and smoked foods.

These studies suggest that diets low in total and saturated fat and cholesterol, and including plenty of whole-grain breads and cereals, fruits and vegetables (including dried beans and peas) decrease the risk of heart disease and may help reduce the risk of cancer.

Gladys Block, Ph.D., and colleagues at the University of California in Berkeley, reviewed a large number of studies that compared the intake of fruits and vegetables and the incidence of cancer. Most of these studies showed a reduced risk of cancer by eating more fruits and vegetables. For most cancer sites, people who ate fewer fruits and vegetables were at twice the risk compared with those who consumed more of these foods, Dr. Block's study found.

Attention was also given to studies by Drs. Kristi Steimetz and John Potter of the University of Minnesota, who reviewed 137 epidemiological studies and concluded that consuming more fruits and vegetables was consistently associated with a reduced risk of cancer.

Dr. Regina Ziegler of NCI's Division of Cancer Etiology has suggested that convincing evidence supports the benefits of fruits and vegetables for the risk of lung cancer. However, she added, these foods cannot substitute for stopping smoking.

Recapping the results of these studies, the press conference was told that higher intakes of fruits and vegetables are associated with a decreased risk of cancer of the esophagus, oral cavity, stomach, colon, rectum, lung and larynx.

In a survey conducted by NCI in 1991, which involved 2,800 adults, it was found that only 23 percent ate five or more servings of fruits and vegetables each day. Men generally ate only three servings, compared with four for women.

The most popular fruits among Americans are apples, bananas, green seedless grapes, strawberries, cantaloupe, peaches, watermelon, oranges, seedless red grapes and lemons. For vegetables, the preference, in order, are iceberg lettuce, carrots, tomatoes, celery, cucumbers, corn, green peppers, broccoli and potatoes.

In March 1992, broccoli made headlines when it was reported that this vegetable contains a powerful weapon against cancer-causing substances, according to Science News.

Paul Talalay and colleagues at the Johns Hopkins School of Medicine in Baltimore have identified a chemical in broccoli as sulforaphane, which seems to stimulate animal and human cells to produce cancer-fighting enzymes. Sulforaphane is probably the most potent protective agent yet discovered, Talalay said.

Researchers have suspected since the mid-1970s that some vegetables confer resistance to cancer, especially the cruciferous vegetables, such as broccoli, brussels sprouts and cabbage.

Murray, Frank; Fruits and Vegetables Extend Our Lifespan, Better Nutrition for Today's Living, Health Watch, October, 1992. This article is reprinted with permission, copyright 1992 by Active Interest Media.

## WHOLE-GRAIN FOODS

There are many wholesome grains. Each one has its own unique flavor, texture and nutritional profile. The diet should include a variety of grains in order to supply the body with maximum nutrition from them.

Grains are mostly used in the making of cereals, flours and flour products. There are both hot and cold whole-grain cereals made from all of the grains. The most popular cereals in the U.S. are made from oats and wheat. All of the grains can be ground into flour for baked goods and for thickening in recipes. Whole-grain breads and cakes are usually tan or brown in color and firm to the touch. Pasta is made from flour, and today there are pasta products made from all of the grains. Corn may be served in the milk stage as a whole-grain or cream-style vegetable. There are many excellent recipes which use grains in preparing main dishes.

The most commonly used grains in the U.S. are wheat, oats, rice, corn, barley and rye. The less familiar grains include buckwheat, amaranth, millet and quinoa. Buckwheat is not really a grain; but, because of its chemical make-up, it is used as a grain. The grains which are very high in nutrition are wheat, oats, quinoa, brown rice, buckwheat and amaranth. Quinoa is the only grain that is a complete protein food because it contains all of the essential amino-acids.

Whole-grains are complex carbohydrates. They supply the body with nutrition and long-sustained energy. The fiber, vitamins and minerals in whole-grains are found in their outer layer. The problem today is that grains (especially wheat and brown rice) are milled or polished in order to shorten the cooking time and to improve both color and texture. The process of polishing the grain removes the outer layer which greatly reduces the nutritional value. For this reason, try to avoid all white, processed foods such as breads, cereals, rice and pasta. To receive maximum nutrition, we should only consume foods made from whole-grains.

Processed grains contribute to malnutrition and obesity by robbing the body of necessary nutrients. Because these foods supply little nutrition, people often feel hungry and have a tendency to overeat. As a result, the body is overfed, overweight and undernourished. People don't realize that often when they feel hungry, the body is calling for nutrition instead of additional calories to be stored as fat. The diet should supply the body with ample calories in the form of highly nutritious foods that will sustain life, health, energy and give a sense of well-being. A diet high in processed foods will not meet these needs. They will only leave the body sick, overweight, tired and hungry. Obesity and malnutrition prepare the body for many forms of sickness and disease.

White, starchy, refined foods don't digest well. They contribute to problems such as colon cancer, diverticulitis, diverticulosis, indigestion and constipation. Processed foods such as white bread, white rice and white pasta lack the fiber which is necessary to move them along the digestive tract and out of the body in a timely manner. Instead, they form a pasty, doughy substance which builds up on the walls of the intestinal tract and clog the system. Food residues remaining in the digestive tract too long rot and putrefy creating problems and sending poisons throughout the system.

Whole-grain foods (complex carbohydrates) help to stabilize blood sugar levels by "burning" or metabolizing slowly in the body and by releasing the sugars from the carbohydrates into the bloodstream over a long period of time. This helps to prevent the highs and lows in blood sugar levels which over a period of time result in diabetes (high blood sugar) and hypoglycemia (low blood sugar). The prolonged release of sugar into the bloodstream also provides the body with energy over a greater period of time rather than a quick burst of energy (high) followed by a sudden drop (low). When refined or processed grains are eaten, they become simple carbohydrates in the body which metabolize rapidly and release food sugars quickly into the bloodstream causing blood sugar highs and lows with their resulting health complications. We can help to eliminate these problems by eating whole-grain foods.

## PROTEIN IN THE DIET
### Beans, Peas, Seeds and Nuts

We often think of protein as a single nutrient, but the dictionary defines protein as any of a class of complex carbohydrates that contain amino-acids as part of their basic structure. Amino-acids are the essential components of protein, and there are many different amino-acids.

Protein is found in all living matter. It is the building block in the cell structure of both plants and animals and is necessary for all life processes in them. Therefore, protein is found in all natural foods to a greater or lesser degree.

Aside from meat and dairy products, the greatest source of protein is found in the food group containing beans, peas, seeds and nuts. Beans and peas contain about the same percentage of protein as meat and about twice as much protein as found in grains. Nuts and seeds are protein-rich but should be used sparingly because of the high oil content.

Beans, peas, seeds and nuts are the embryos of plants, and in them are stored all of the protein, vitamins, minerals etc. necessary to sustain the new plant life. When we eat these plant embryos, our bodies are nourished by the concentrated nutrients which they contain.

The main function of protein in the body is to build and repair cells as they wear out. Protein also helps to regulate body processes and supply energy if enough fats and carbohydrates have not been consumed. If more protein is taken in than needed, it is broken down and stored as body fat, not as a reserve supply of protein.

Sufficient and complete protein will be supplied in a vegetarian diet if it includes a variety of foods, enough calories and a variety of protein foods daily to supply all of the amino-acids necessary for good health.

Many studies now indicate that most Americans consume too much protein in the form of meat and dairy products and not enough fresh fruits, vegetables, whole grains, legumes (beans and peas) and seeds and nuts. The consequences of both factors have been poor health, sickness and disease on a large scale.

## FLESH FOODS IN THE DIET

1. Harmful Substances in Meat

    Chemicals, hormones and harmful additives are often included in the feed for animals to fatten and for health. About 80 percent of all pesticides used in the U.S. are concentrated upon wheat, corn, soybean and cotton crops which make up the bulk of cattle feed (Hitchcox, Lee; Long Life Now, Celestial Hearts, 1996 p. 59). These chemicals, which are passed on to those who eat the meat, have many harmful effects. The hormones in the meat have been found to produce unnatural, rapid growth and early puberty in children, and the dyes, preservatives and detoxification substances used in meat processing are all toxic to humans.

2. <u>Contamination of Meat by Sick and Diseased Animals</u>
The sickness and disease of animals are passed on to those who consume the meat. Mad Cow Disease, E. Coli, salmonella, campylobacter, mercury, lead etc. are all transmitted from contaminated meat to humans.

3. <u>Transportation of Animals</u>
Transportation is often unsanitary and crowded with sick animals.

4. <u>Slaughtering of Animals</u>
The animals are often in a state of hysteria when being killed. The hysteria causes physical reactions which release excessive and harmful chemicals, hormones and enzymes into the system causing the blood and the meat to be toxic.

5. <u>Meat Processing</u>
Poor quality control in unsanitary meat processing and packaging plants make meat unfit for human consumption.

6. <u>Quality Control of Meat Products</u>
Cancerous, tumerous and tuberculosis laden meat often pass inspection for market.

7. <u>Sale of Meat Products</u>
Old and outdated meat is often dyed, repackaged, relabeled as to the expiration date and sold.

8. <u>Uric Acid in Meat</u>
Uric acid is a white crystalline substance found in urine which is made up of waste materials filtered from the blood by the kidneys. The uric acid in meat causes it to be addictive. When a person begins to eliminate meat from his diet, he may feel tired, weak or sick for awhile as he is going through withdrawal symptoms from the uric acid in the meat.

Uric acid builds up in the muscles and joints causing them to stiffen, become painful and lose range of motion. Uric acid build-up is also found in joints effected by gout, in kidney stones and in gallstones.

9. <u>Lack of Fiber in Meat and Meat Products</u>
Fiber is a substance found only in plants; therefore, the dietary fiber that we need can only be supplied by plant foods. The plant foods which are highest in dietary fiber are fruits and vegetables. The lack of fiber containing foods in the diet is the main cause of colon cancer. In the digestive system, fiber helps to move the food through the intestines in a timely manner. It absorbs excess moisture and toxic waste materials in the system and helps to excrete them from the body. The work of the fiber helps to shorten the time that the body is exposed to toxins and waste materials. Flesh foods and animal products have no fiber. Therefore, they move slowly and often remain in the intestines too long where they ferment and putrefy producing cancer causing compounds and sending poisons throughout the system.

10. <u>Fat, Cholesterol, Protein and Chemicals in Meat</u>
The saturated fat, cholesterol, concentrated protein and chemical residues in meat are threats to our health. The following information is only a little of the information available on this topic. The fat and cholesterol build up inside the arteries contribute to atherosclerosis which is the main cause of death from cardiovascular and heart disease. Conclusive studies around the world are linking the high fat and animal protein of a meat and dairy based diet to cancer, especially breast, prostate and colon cancers. Research is now showing that osteoporosis is not caused by a lack of calcium in the diet but by an excess of protein. The overload of protein from meat and dairy products in the body causes the blood to become acidic. The body tries to

neutralize the acid by pulling calcium from the bones. This calcium is lost by being excreted from the body in the urine. As a result of this repeated process, over a period of time, the bones become deficient in calcium resulting in osteoporosis which is a state of weak, porous, brittle bones. In countries, such as China, where the people have eaten a plant-based diet for years, osteoporosis is rare because protein in plant foods is not acid-forming as is protein from meat and animal products. Regarding chemicals, both plant and animal foods contain harmful chemicals unless they are organic. However, the chemicals and pesticides on produce are usually of a lesser amount and potency in comparison to those found in meat products.

11. Man's Original and Perfect Diet

    Flesh food was not part of God's original diet for man. Man's original diet was a vegetarian diet (Gen. 1:29). It was only after the flood that God permitted flesh food in man's diet (Gen. 9:1). In heaven, when God has restored all things to His original plan, there will be no killing of animals to supply meat for food. Man and animals will have a vegetarian diet.

## THE IMPORTANCE OF PROPER FOOD COMBINING

Proper food combining assures better and more efficient digestion of food and the absorption of its nutrients by the body. The study of digestion deals with the chemical changes that food undergoes from the time it enters the mouth until it leaves the body. Digestion involves the type and amount of food eaten and its digestive requirements.

All foods are predominately either carbohydrates (sugars and starches), protein or fats and oils. There are many foods in each group. Each group and each food within that group has its own characteristics (chemical structure) and digestive requirements.

The requirements are those things or conditions necessary for proper digestion. For example, each food is processed in a certain period of time, requires a specific enzyme and can be digested only in the proper acid/alkaline environment. Only those foods which are compatible in characteristics and digestive requirements should be eaten together. When we combine foods having different characteristics, we form unnatural food combinations which place difficult and often impossible demands (requirements) upon the body. As a result, the brain becomes confused, the digestive system is upset and indigestion occurs.

Indigestion is difficulty in digesting food, and it results in the food being either partially digested or not digested at all. The partially digested or undigested food lies in the stomach and intestines where it decays and ferments. Instead of nutrients, the blood absorbs poisons from the decaying food and carries them throughout the body setting it up for sickness and disease. The decaying food in the stomach and intestines contributes to ulcers, colitis, colon cancer, nervous bowel syndrome, diverticulitis, diverticulosis and other gastro-intestinal disorders. Proper food combining helps to eliminate these complications of indigestion.

Indigestion is a waste of food and it robs the body of nutrition as we receive little nutrition from partially digested food and none from that which is totally undigested. The continued loss of nutrients due to ongoing indigestion leads to serious malnutrition.

Indigestion overtaxes the body, prematurely wears out the digestive organs and uses up the body's vital forces unnecessarily. Proper food combining helps to simplify and lighten the body's work of digestion.

People who suffer from indigestion often experience heartburn, bloating, constipation, diarrhea, stomach cramps, bad breath, foul-smelling stools and flatulence (gas). The gases formed in the stomach and intestines are toxic and harmful to the body. Often, instead of taking antacids and other medicines, people need only to combine their foods correctly.

In summary, improperly combining the foods which we eat causes indigestion. Indigestion is more than an uncomfortable feeling, it is a physical disorder which has many ill-effects upon the body. We can help to avoid indigestion and its effects by eating together foods that combine well in the digestive system. We may not be able to form the best combinations of our food at all times, but every good combination is of benefit. Two excellent books to read on the subject of food combining are: (1) Food Combining Made Easy by Herbert M. Shelton and (2) The Complete Book of Food Combining: New Approach to Healthy Eating by Jan Dries and Inge Dries.

# Food Combining Chart

**Food Friends & Foes**

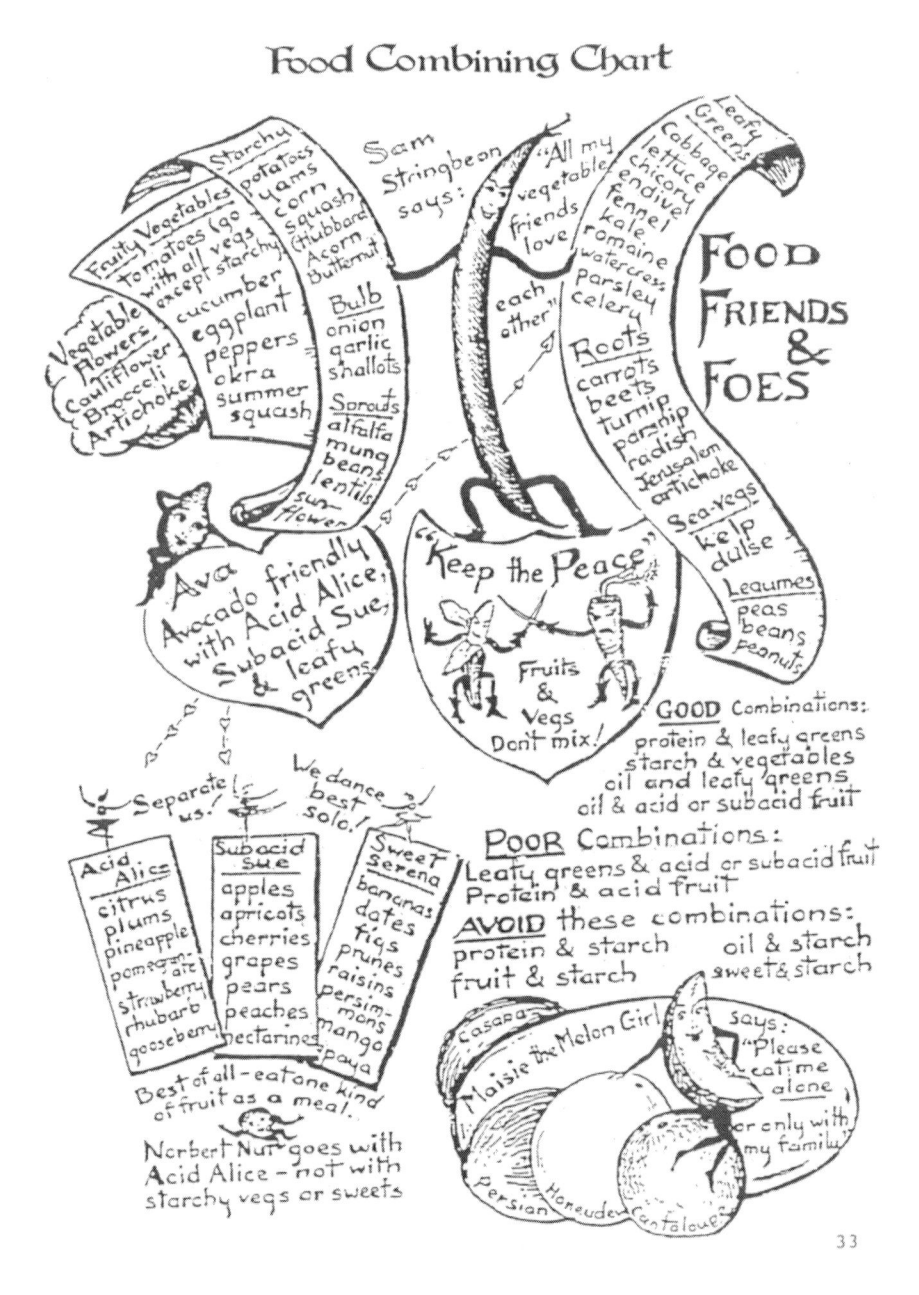

Starchy: potatoes, yams, corn, squash (Chubbard, Acorn, Butternut)

Fruity Vegetables (go with all vegs except starchy): Tomatoes, cucumber, eggplant, peppers, okra, summer squash

Vegetable Flowers: Cauliflower, Broccoli, Artichoke

Bulb: onion, garlic, shallots

Sprouts: alfalfa, mung bean, lentils, sunflower

Sam Stringbean says: "All my vegetable friends love each other"

Leafy Greens: Cabbage, lettuce, chicory, endive, fennel, kale, romaine, watercress, parsley, celery

Roots: carrots, beets, turnip, parsnip, radish, Jerusalem artichoke

Sea-vegs: kelp, dulse

Legumes: peas, beans, peanuts

Ava Avocado friendly with Acid Alice, Subacid Sue & leafy greens

"Keep the Peace" — Fruits & Vegs Don't mix!

**GOOD Combinations:**
protein & leafy greens
starch & vegetables
oil and leafy greens
oil & acid or subacid fruit

**POOR Combinations:**
Leafy greens & acid or subacid fruit
Protein & acid fruit

**AVOID these combinations:**
protein & starch
fruit & starch
oil & starch
sweet & starch

Separate us!   We dance best solo!

Acid Alice: citrus, plums, pineapple, pomegranate, strawberry, rhubarb, gooseberry

Subacid Sue: apples, apricots, cherries, grapes, pears, peaches, nectarines

Sweet Serena: bananas, dates, figs, prunes, raisins, persimmons, mango, papaya

Best of all - eat one kind of fruit as a meal!

Norbert Nut goes with Acid Alice - not with starchy vegs or sweets

Maisie the Melon Girl says: "Please eat me alone or only with my family" — Casaba, Persian, Honeydew, Cantaloupe

Hoehn, Herman; Food Friends & Foes, Hoehn Research Library, Grand Forks, Canada.

## 7. TEMPERANCE

The dictionary defines *temperate* as (1) moderate, not excessive; (2) moderate; not inclined to eat or drink to excess, especially alcoholic beverages; (3) calm, restrained, self-controlled in actions, speech etc.

The dictionary defines *temperance* as (1) being temperate; (2) habitual moderation, the practice of avoidance of extremes; (3) practice of total abstinence from the use of intoxicating liquors. Temperance, when used in reference to intoxicating liquors, though originally used in moderation, has come to mean total abstinence. Total abstinence means going without.

In general, temperance means voluntary self-restraint and moderation in eating and drinking, in conduct, in expression and in the taking of pleasures.

The dictionary defines *intemperate* as (1) not temperate or moderate, excessive; (2) drinking too much alcoholic liquor.

Intemperance leads to harmful dependencies of which the negative effects upon human health have been well-documented by medical science. For those with such dependencies, of which drugs, alcohol and tobacco are only a few, a plan of temperance offers something better by providing a positive, practical and effective alternative.

The dictionary defines temperance, but it does not tell how to develop it in one's life. The problem being that humans have not the strength within themselves to do so. True temperance is God's plan for man, whereby man's habits, disposition and character may be reformed for the better. The Christian plan of temperance is one of strength and self-control through Christ Jesus. It enables the believer to resist and to overcome the temptations of intemperance, addictions and dependencies.

# INTEMPERATE EATING HABITS

Temperance in eating is the discipline of choosing healthy foods and eating them in moderation. Most people enjoy eating but need to remember that not only is eating to be a pleasure, but the food is to sustain life and health by supplying nutrients for building and repairing the body. In fact, food is our best form of medicine. What we eat and how much we eat on a daily basis helps to determine the quality of our overall health. Good foods produce good blood and sound health. Continually eating nutrient-poor food leads to malnutrition, sickness and disease. The amount of food required varies with each individual and his particular lifestyle. However, when we indulge in overeating and in eating too frequently, the stomach and digestive organs are overworked, the system becomes clogged and the excess calories are stored as fat.

Often, when the body has finished the heavy task of trying to digest the overload of food, it may feel tired, faint and sluggish because it is exhausted. Unfortunately, people sometimes mistake these feelings for hunger and eat more food when what the tired and overworked stomach and digestive organs are really signaling for is rest. In such cases, to fast or to eat very lightly for a meal or two allows the needed rest. At times, the digestive system cannot handle the overload of food, and the food that is either partially digested or completely undigested decays in the digestive tract leading to serious health problems. We may safely say that poor food choices and overeating produce sickness, disease and premature death instead of good health.

Appetite and taste are not safe guides for selecting healthy foods or for necessarily determining the amount that should be eaten. Through wrong habits of eating, the appetite has become poorly trained and often misleads us by demanding both foods and amounts of food which are not good for us. These wrong habits can be changed by determination and effort. Not all foods agree with everyone, but nature has supplied us with such a great variety of foods that each person may choose what best suits him. As for the amount eaten, one should never eat more than he feels he needs or until he is uncomfortable.

Food should be selected and prepared by one who realizes that he occupies a most important position, seeing that good food which is properly prepared is required for good health and long life. Abstemiousness in diet is greatly rewarded with mental, physical and moral vigor.

## 8. TRUST IN GOD

When we have done all that we know to do to promote good health or cure disease, we trust God for the rest. He is our Creator and our Great Physician. He understands our frame and knows both our needs and what is best for us. He is more than able to care for us.

Trust in God is the result of a growing, loving, obedient relationship with Him. It is the belief and calm assurance that regardless of the circumstances, He knows what is best for us, He is personally with us and He will never leave us.

Our trust does not mean receiving all that we in our limited knowledge and understanding ask for. Trust means submitting our wills to God in acceptance of His perfect will in our lives. Trust means that God's will becomes our will as we allow Him to live His life through us to His honor, glory and our subsequent salvation.

God loves us and His promises in scripture are true. The same power that Christ exercised as He walked the earth is in His word, and it is still with us today. We need only to accept and obey. His loving principles are to govern every aspect of our being; the mental, the physical and the spiritual.

# Notes

# Notes

# PERSONAL HEALTH CHART

| | Sun. | Mon. | Tues. | Wed. | Thurs. | Fri. | Sat. |
|---|---|---|---|---|---|---|---|
| **Sleep**<br>Time to bed<br>No. of hours of sleep | | | | | | | |
| **Exercise**<br>Type _____<br>Amount of time | | | | | | | |
| **Air - Sunlight**<br>Amount of time | | | | | | | |
| **Nutrition**<br>No. of fruits<br>No. of vegetables<br>No. of whole grains | | | | | | | |
| **Water**<br>No. of 8 oz. glasses | | | | | | | |
| **Quiet Time for Self**<br>Amount of time | | | | | | | |
| **Personal Devotions**<br>Amount of time | | | | | | | |

# Health Diary

_____ Date _____

_____

_____

_____

_____

_____

_____

_____ Date _____

_____

_____

_____

_____

_____

_____

# Diary

Date

Date

# *Diary*

Date

Date

# *Diary*

**Date**

**Date**

# *Diary*

Date

Date

# *Diary*

Date

Date

# Diary

Date

Date

# Diary

Date

Date

# Diary

Date

Date

# Diary

Date

Date